The Man With My Face

The Man With My Face

...

Poems by Jennifer Tseng

Copyright ©2005 by Jennifer Tseng

All rights reserved. No part of this book may be used or reproduced in any matter without written permission.

Library of Congress Control Number 2005922070

ISBN: 1-889876-17-8 (paper)

The publication of this book is funded through a generous grant from The Ford Foundation. Additional support provided by The Rockefeller Brothers Fund, The New York State Council on the Arts and The Jerome Foundation in celebration of the Jerome Hill Centennial and in recognition of the valuable cultural contributions of artists to society.

Cover and book design by Purple Gate Design
www.purplegatedesign.com

Cover art by Amanda Tseng
adoptedjane@yahoo.com

Published in the United States of America by The Asian American Writers' Workshop, 16 West 32nd Street, Suite 10A, New York, NY 10001. Email us at desk@aaww.org. The Asian American Writers' Workshop is a nonprofit literary organization devoted to the creation, development, publication and dissemination of Asian American literature.

for my father, mother and sister

CONTENTS

· one

Red Handkerchief	13
Autobiography of an Immigrant	16
My Father on Poetry	18
Alien of Extraordinary Ability at Sea	19
Nostomania	20
Immigrant Divorcé	21
In the Absence of Dictionaries	22
Life as Foreign Film	23
A Picture Language	24
For My Father	25

two

Trees	29
Arms	32
Desire	33
Dark-eyed Junco	34
Tender	35
The Vanishing	36
When the Living Say No	39
The Human Part	41
Liars	42
Possible Body	44
Against Einstein	46

To the Thing Itself	48
Another Immigrant in Love	50
Exotic Winter	53
Devotions	54
Loves My Mother Taught Me	56
Prayer	57
Flame	58
To Be Made	59
The World Before the World	61
Enter the Dark	64

three

Record Player in an Immigrant Household	69
A Brief History of *We* and *Us*	70
The Father and the Daughter	71
Musical Lexicons	72
New Old	73
Mother's Violin	75
Father's Violin	76
Indecipherable Guide to Strange Birds	77

acknowledgments 80

one

12.

RED HANDKERCHIEF

I.

I am making this poem for you
in the manner of a handkerchief.
To shake at the sky, to fold
as your ship leaves the shore.

Red for the blood that races
distance. Veins arbitrary, blood
yours. Square for the shape
of limits and four-fold returns.

Cut from your mother's dress,
its weave consoles you. Palm
sugar in the hem, for the sea
is harsh and you will be hungry.

If I asked, you would claim
not to need it.
Yet there it is in your pocket.
There it is hidden.

Rain. You lean on the prow
and dream of me: child with a mind
like your own, child who might
write you a love poem.

How can you know that I'll speak
a stranger's language?
My poems more bright red
scraps than words you love?

Fever.   The sailors blow their noses
with their hands. Your hands are clean.
The red cloth, clean. But even in my poem,
mucus, raindrops, tears, the sea, darken it.

II.

I am making this poem for myself
so that I might watch you
sail the long sea toward me.
Fifty years and what have you lost?

Red for the complicated body,
veins arbitrary, blood ours.
A square resembles the four
of us eating at a table.

The weave of my grandmother's dress.
Tears that perfumed her manly face
and hands. Sweat from your endless
forehead, rinsed clean by a storm.

If you asked, I would claim not to need it.
Yet here it is in my hand, here
it is written. I have wanted to be
this poem in another language.

I have wanted to be the handkerchief:
red hidden in the dark
of your suit, an organ working,
red for the black duration.

AUTOBIOGRAPHY OF AN IMMIGRANT

My birthplace is incidental.
Never forget your Mother Country.

Our place was nowhere, nothing but dirt.
Our province was known for its temples.

The way my mother ran the house was backwards.
You don't taste fish like that here.

I don't remember what my father said.
We memorized everything our father said.

Chinese don't marry for love.
My father and mother loved each other very much.

Chinese families are unified; nothing can break them.
I haven't talked to my sister since I was twelve.

I spoke every language fluently, top of my class.
My English is terrible, I forget my Chinese.

Chinese children obey their parents' orders.
I ran away from home.

Your daddy is a very cautious person.
I left my country at night; I hid from the government.

The sea voyage took three weeks.
I walked on the water.

There was nothing special about my journey.
Our ship was lost at sea.

The barrels flooded after days
Of rain. Oranges spilled

Across the dark deck, many fell in
To the black water. It was a catastrophe.

Our hunger, such as you can't imagine.

MY FATHER ON POETRY

You write of revolution,
loss of language.
The smell of ammunition
in the night air afterwards.
How it resembled a festival.

You saw nothing.
It was I who burned history
behind the Shandong house.
I with a flame in my hand,
you with a poem.

Between us, two poems.
Yours: war's night air on a page.

Mine: a fire, elsewhere.

ALIEN OF EXTRAORDINARY ABILITY AT SEA

Scholar not sailor, he flinched
at the sound of the others
coughing up phlegm.
Like his mind his flinching,
fine as salt from the sea.

So his passing began.
His sinuous body stood
for labor, its color for sun.
His mind, flinch and salt
stayed hidden.

Like brothers, the words
on paper looked the same.
The sailors did not write, but spoke
instead. In speech he found
their sounds diverged.

Despite his aversion to sweat,
he is like the salt.
Rock, granule, powder, dust,
a potent taste that none
but the sea can soften.

NOSTOMANIA

On his list of forbidden
pleasures, somewhere close
to women. Beauty banned
from orderly house and mind. The garage
was different, was the place
he hung pictures of women
with faces like his own.
Shandong its analogue...

Dark room in the back
of the mind, filled with
things once known,
gone, supple.

IMMIGRANT DIVORCÉ

One wife spoke the language
of an alien world. In our house,
it was always tomorrow.

One wife spoke the language
of a world I had known. In our house,
it was always yesterday.

A stranger's life, a life forgotten.
Never today—all the time travel.

IN THE ABSENCE OF DICTIONARIES

The words he used were stones.

He carried three in his pocket:
fruit   rain   earth
He had an orchard, he wanted her to know
these things mattered to him.

He brought her an apple and placed it
next to *fruit*. He put a cup
on the steps and collected rain.
He filled a bowl with dirt from the yard.

She began to understand *fruit*
as a red thing, *rain*
as a half-empty cup, *earth*
as the darkness that fits in a bowl.

In the end they were buried
by objects and stones.
Their bones, no nursery
rhyme bones, all of them broken.

LIFE AS FOREIGN FILM

He's been away from his country so long,
he can't take the twelve-hour flight
without wanting a sandwich.
Nights he dreams his return in English.
Mornings he strolls the sunny sidewalk
of his American neighborhood, the small English
dictionary looking like cigarettes in his pant pocket.
He eats lunch with his green-eyed wife, the words
for *duck*, *squab* and *pheasant* fly off.

America is full of people like him.
Immigrants dreaming in English
with subtitles, of faraway countries.
If only they dreamed the same country,
subtitled the same lost language. They could,
these Americans, form their own society,
a society against loneliness,
devoted to memory, language,
the translation of dreams.

A PICTURE LANGUAGE

When I say it, you don't understand.
Your eyes hold rain, a lost animal,
darkness and miles to go. When I draw:

> 大 man.

> 水 water.

> 日 sun.

I see a man
with a lantern in one hand,
a lamb in the other.

FOR MY FATHER

At the last I have to wonder if people
like you have a history of ending like this:
Alone in a strange land, strange language.
No love. All ambition. Your family, afraid
of leaving you, tricks you into leaving
them. The meek are impossibly brilliant.

Certainly during waking hours, you're the brilliant
one, the man with the overseas jobs, the man people
pay money to see, the man who prefers to leave
small things behind in search of greatness. This
you believe you do for others. Yet you're afraid
it will never be enough. Inevitably, the language

you find, will never make sense with your first language.
You make the choice without knowing. Your brilliance
is the kind with arrows, sky. It's grass you're afraid
of, the dark sacks slung over the shoulders of people
like yourself. Smallness. *Don't let it come to this.*
Don't let me be the held one, but the one leaving.

You dream while your loved ones plan your leaving.
Tired of your strong arms, your aim, their language
is written in sleep. All night. All quiet. Finally this
is the way they sing themselves free. So many brilliant
schemes hatched in the dark. These are the very people
who cut the grass, boil the water and sleep, unafraid.

Consider the soldier's twenty-year-old wife, afraid
of widowhood, or the sojourner's for whom leaving
was never a possibility. We all know that people
pity the left. There is proof of this in language:
Abandoned: the poor one left. *Adventurer*: the brilliant
one gone. Yet some of the left must have used this

to their advantage. Clever in their sadness. This
was Mother's genius when she said, *Yes I'm afraid
of course, but I think you should go. You're brilliant
dear, you always have been. As soon as you leave
the children and I will follow.* Nothing in her language
surprised you. Then you stopped trusting people.

This was your story. In time my love would leave.
Unafraid he said, *You left yourself.* I knew the language
brilliant, meek. At last we were part of the same people.

two

28

TREES

One summer he planted a tree.
It was young,
small as a rose bush.
We were intent on watching it.
We were young,
we wanted the fruit to come.

Father brought the coffee can outside,
paced between the tree and the backyard spigot.
We liked to watch him fill the can,
feed water to the little tree.
We liked to see the brown soil
blacken beneath his fingers.

Young trees keep their fruit inside
for so long. You have to stay with them
for years before they'll bear it.

When the first pear came
we forgot about the water,
the soil and the man
with the coffee can.
We could already taste its sweetness
through the hard, green skin.
It hung there new, like so
many curves we recognized.

Don't touch
he said
don't touch.

We listened at first, we obeyed
because it was small then
easier to resist.
But later we saw
its size would fill up our hands.
At night when he went away
we held it.

Finally the yellow ink took over,
the flesh was soft,
we became gentle.
Father decided it was time
to pluck it,
he decided it was
time to eat.

Mother brought out the special plate,
the red one mottled with Chinese birds.
He placed the yellow pear on the red plate,
divided the fruit with a knife.

It lay there open like a flower,
a pale tropical thing with four
petals, keen with the smell of sugar.
Each one dripping juice, almost tears,
each one riven from the others,
so yellow against the red birds.

Choose one,
he said.
And we knew he would watch
to see which one we chose.
The old story echoed in the air,
he did not have to speak
to tell it. The story of the child
with the most honor
the one who saves the best
for her mother.
All of us fight
for the smallest piece.

Soon the fruit is gone,
eaten under his watchful eye.
Time to wait for the next one.
Mother rinses the plate,
shines the birds with her swift cloth.

Now he has cut the tree down.
He says it interferes with the plumbing.
Too many roots.
Mother is a bird flying.
Sister sends me fruit in the mail:
apricots, cranberries, apples, plums.
We are young, small,
hungry as girls, hiding
our fruit in the cupboards.

ARMS

In the darkened closet Sister
sleeps, her hair against my skin.

Eyes closed, hair unpinned, both
our nightgowns torn. Here was safety

we'd pretend, our pillows clean
and soft on the wooden floor.

One trying to be Mother, one
breathing the dust of our dresses in.

During the day in the bright yard
I pedaled my bike on the porch.

Remember you used to stand
in the grass with your arms out?

All day you stood waiting
for birds to land on your arms.

Sometimes at twilight, they landed.
I could not think of joining you.

Sister, I sat on my bike, watching
your arms, jealous of the birds.

DESIRE

This desire
is a kind of sleeping,
a kind of forgetting,
a lost childhood.

I begin to see myself as a skin cave,
dark, without details.
You and I are there having tea,
stirring the tea with our bones,
each with our own bones.

I would drink your reflection
but I cannot find the cup,
I cannot find my hands.

DARK-EYED JUNCO

Though the guidebooks call you common:
brown bird, brown eyes, brown sheen,
each sooty silky cell to me seems
swallowed, lost in the rest.

(Where is the eye?) So dark
it shines, look
closely I will find it,
I am used to this confusion.

You are my kind
of beauty, no matter
how often you appear
to fill the trees

like common leaves,
turn blue skies black
with flocks, your dreams
invisible in this dark,

American night.
You could be the most common bird in the hemisphere.
I would still look for you.

TENDER

Three horses in a field: white in the distance,
black chewing grass and the sooty one
closest to the fence, watching me.

The child I love was born
with a crooked finger, no injury, still
I'm careful with that one.

When guests arrived my father would shake
their hands, my mother would smile
and cough, my sister would hide.

I put the plums in a bowl as much
to display them as to keep them somewhere.
One, blacker than the rest, I ate immediately.

Sooty horse, crooked finger, hidden sister, blackest plum.
Animals and body parts, relatives and fruit, of the tough
and distant many, you are that one.

THE VANISHING

I.

There was a door opening
in the middle of the night.
There was light and a can
of sweetened condensed milk,
open, like a moon on the last shelf.
Twice nightly she would kneel down,
stick her finger in the milk moon
and eat. The walk back to her room,
dark and in the morning always
two drops of milk on the floor.
Milk that had dripped from her
mouth, to her chin, to the floor.

After the war, they had the refrigerator
but no electric. A few times
in her child sleep she forgot this,
came to the kitchen to take milk
like before. When she opened
the door, the dark in the room
stayed there. Her hand, reaching
for the milk, found seven burlap
sacks of rice and a cardboard box
filled with her father's old diaries.

II.

Of course my father and I
would go places together.
He carried me on his shoulders
at the bank, above the strangers,
above the money changing hands.
He drove me to piano lessons
like a chauffeur, while I sat
in the back seat practicing.
My hands, my tiny horses
galloped for miles.

Later, I would run into him
in public places. That to me
was an end in itself.
I had gone to the post office
to mail him a letter.
He was at the counter.
I knew his checked jacket.
I knew the back of his head.
I wouldn't have to send the letter.

He turned to go and looked at me,
his eyes held mine as they might
a stranger's. Not wanting
to have to tell him who I was,
I stood in line to buy stamps
and watched him leave, the letter
needing to be sent after all.

III.

On his daily walk through the woods
the man has an appetite: for the many
colored eyes of the leaves, red orange,
red green, the way the sun
scents the branches.

In winter when the man comes
home, it's dark. As if half
his day is lost. His path
through the woods, lost.
Though his eyes adjust, he's afraid.
Where are the leaves? Gone, brown,
brittle underfoot. Nothing is the same.
In the snow, in the dark,
patience replaces his appetite.

IV.

The end of pleasure was like that.
Except there was no war, no door
opening in the middle of the night.
Milk was plentiful. You did not grow old.
Patience was easy and didn't matter.
That end was just that.
No reason. No return.
Pleasure ended.

WHEN THE LIVING SAY NO

I wish I could have lost you
some other way.
Lightning and the edge of a lake,
faulty brakes, a drunk driver.
I wish for equations that don't
have *no* at their heart.

Instead I wake to remember
you're still alive.
What made you disappear,
nothing to do with disasters
or recklessness. I have to think that.
The end was in you all along,
foisted upon us like a mistake
from a previous life.
No matter how careful I'd been,
you'd have vanished.

When I think of all the people
who have lost their loves
to fires, drownings, plagues,
I'm ashamed.
How can *no* be worse than death?

When I hear your voice say it
I try to think:
At least he is breathing,
at least he can still say the word.
I try to think of it this way.
But I can't.

THE HUMAN PART

Your departure was very faint, very human.
In the beginning, I could not hear it
because the sound of a body leaving can

trick the ear, the way an expert surgeon
heals. You were never broken, never cut.
Your departure was very faint, very human,

a pitch so high, only dogs would run
and bark toward its musical height.
Just as the sound of a body leaving can

resemble cleaving and some sleepers can
confuse blue morning with grey twilight,
your departure was very faint, very human.

The sound of a body arriving can't contain
your exit song (tone grey, pulse quiet)
but the sound of a body leaving can.

Now that I know its sound, I avoid everyone.
I don't want to hear anyone's body depart
because the sound of a body leaving can
be your departure, very faint, very human.

LIARS

I.

As children we screamed that our pants were on fire.
We jumped on the bed pretending to be monkeys.

When Boo Boo our rat died, I covered his cage.
Shhh...don't look in there, he's sleeping.

I told the neighbors my name was Lisa.
No one could find me when I was lost.

The nuns asked Claudine if we were sisters.
Claudine said, *Yes...fraternal twins...parents divorced...*

I misunderstood time because the tree in our yard
    bloomed so much.
Mother used the words *false* and *spring*.

At a gas station in Redding, Diane told Evelyn the
    soap was honey.
She let it fall into her hand, a wet golden swirl and
    then she let Evelyn lick it.

Afraid of poverty and jail, I cheated at Monopoly.
I slipped pink and gold dollars under my leg.

II.

Now innocent and terrible love, let me
Make you a liar from my childhood:

You have dreamed your life was an animal's life.
You have hidden that which was missing.

You have uttered strange names in self-description.
You have longed for brotherhood.

You have shown your blossoms too late, too soon.
You have sought honey in desolate places.

Human and ordinary one that I loved,
Afraid you would lose, you were like all liars.

POSSIBLE BODY

After she falls, heavy on land,
his eye follows her seaward.

His hands in her hair are stones
in the swimmer's pocket, mines

in a clean wet field. Her hands
sink when she finds them.

At night she reclines in a blue bath,
dreams the water is a sky.

She has tried to be clean before,
she knows the slow descent

of her own drowning. Hands
in her hair, sky overwhelming.

Still she fills the bath each night,
a salt bath deep as her knees.

She is drowning in possible water.
Water takes so many forms,

wrought with reflections. At night
when she's alone, the bath holds both

a picture of the girl drowning
and a picture of her sailing to safety.

Her body at once a raft, a weight.
The thing that pins her down,

the thing that might carry her.

AGAINST EINSTEIN
for PJK

Even now, so late
in the twentieth century,
I understand early obsessions
with finite spaces,
absolute time.

If I'm writing this on a train,
does the line to follow fall
one quarter of an inch
from the last, or two
miles later
depending on the observer
and speed of the train?

How much time exists
between lines?

Despite my intentions,
the reader like a stranger on the platform
sees a new distance.

And if the reader is you
what distance will you observe
in these lines, standing
on a platform in some other city,
waiting for another love to arrive?

The year is 1905,
the past has just been set free
by an anonymous patent clerk
with words. The old
men are up in arms,
afraid of the uncaged feeling
they have when they read.

I see myself among them,
the scientists in decline,
our suits of fear out of fashion,
papers outmoded, theories surpassed.

We are dreaming backwards
and forward to the unattainable
state of rest,
horrified by the idea

that the distance we thought
so hard to close
is immeasurable.

TO THE THING ITSELF

As a child I saw the appliqué bird
on the mailman's chest as a hat.
Wings the crown, head the brim, eye
never part of the simple shape's
equation. Tiny eagle, copy of the thing
our mailman wore for protection.

Yet in this world there can be no protection
from the elements that wreck a bird
stamp's canceled ink. It bleeds across the thing
we call envelope, that plain paper hat
with the triangle flap, holder of words, shaper
of what we see on the outside, our eyes

oblivious to content. What was it my small eye
sought then? Some mimetic form of protection
or the man himself? The familiar shape
repeated itself on his chest, sleeve. Never a bird
but an echo. Never an eagle but his hat.
I looked and looked but could not see the thing

that others had intended, the thing
that others knew meant "x." Where their eyes
saw "American eagle," mine saw Big John's hat.
Who among us needs protection?
Children? Presidents? Postmen? Birds?
Worse than the elements that wreck a shape:

Years later in a post office parking lot I see the old shape
painted on the sides of a hundred trucks. One thing
suddenly certain: the fleet of trucks is a flock of birds.
Oh. And I can't go back. My sorry eye
has been damaged and healed, the protection
offered by a single experience, by one man's hat,

altered by vastness, numbers, weight. Hats
are birds now. You can tell me how to see the shape
of your face, chest, hands. But I can't protect
you from the field that surrounds them. The thing
that stood still and rested, was shade for the eyes
of a man, that hat has become a bird.

It was not the shape that changed, but my eye.
No offense to the thing itself. What was hat
is bird...There in the air, your protection.

ANOTHER IMMIGRANT IN LOVE

He spent most of his time in the downstairs den, building replicas of houses and rooms. He never built entire towns, never a church or a general store, never a library. His neighborhood block, with its five candy-colored houses, resembled the one he saw through their picture window. The rooms he built from memory: boys' sleeping quarters at a church camp in Fresno, kitchen like the one his mother had. The boys' room was filled with stained mattresses and the kitchen was empty. When he was not in the den painting houses or mixing the grey substance he had concocted for the roads, he was out driving the quiet streets in search of materials. He bought chicken wire for the window grates, fishing line for the telephone wires, artificial turf for the lawns.

One day when the man was busy painting a shutter black, a tiny girl walked out of the lemon-colored house, carrying a book in her hand. He was surprised to see her but he didn't show it. Instead he began talking to her as if he'd been waiting for her ever since the day he'd been born in Brazil. *What are you reading?* the man asked, though clearly the book was not a story at all, but several postage stamps glued together to look like a book. *I'm just carrying the book, I'm not reading it*, she said. She wore a red sundress and her black hair was in braids. *What are you doing?* she asked. *That's a good question*, the man answered.

The tiny girl and the lonely man talked for hours. She asked him questions and he told her things he had never even told his wife. When the sun went down and the man and the girl found themselves in the dark, the girl said, *It's my dinnertime.* And she disappeared into the lemon-colored house. He could have peered inside one of the plastic windows to investigate, but he resisted.

For the next several months, the tiny girl reappeared, wearing the same red dress, holding the same fake book. She let him carry her in the pocket of his robe when his wife was home, so that they could be together always. The man's wife noticed that he seemed happier, but she had no idea about the pocket-sized girl. His wife encouraged him to work on his models. She thought he needed to find himself.

One day the girl had a present for the man. She had sewn tiny coverlets for two of his stained mattresses. They were the color of raspberries, laced with gold thread. *One for you and one for me,* she said. *For when you come to visit and we take a nap.* Being in love with the girl hurt the man because he also loved his wife. He felt torn in half and often wished he could make himself small enough to inhabit the model world he had created. Other times he dreamed the girl was the same size he was and still other times he wanted to walk out into the night with the girl in his pocket and never come back.

In order to save his marriage, he decided to destroy the things he had made. Because he could not bear the thought of setting fire to the girl's body, he dismantled the houses carefully before throwing them into the flames. Afraid she might be trapped inside, he pried the roofs off slowly. But she was already gone.

EXOTIC WINTER

On these snow-covered roads
the Eskimo look of her face,
serious and clean, makes winter
into setting, yet real, still chilling.

It's always the same story—
a man who finds her in the dark
as if she were part night, part cold,
one hundred words for snow inside her.

Six long books about darkness,
the green of Northern lights inscribed.
Sky's secret kept in her secretive mouth,
an ice song, not like old music.

He thinks she was built to endure this
sky full of darkness for days,
waiting with stars
in her eyes as guides.

Months he thinks she'll keep on,
one hand warmed by the fire
the other lighting it.
Snow everywhere.

His wife's pregnant again,
business failing. Totemic she appears
in the harshest light: that Chinese girl
God sent to make everything right.

DEVOTIONS

I was swimming the pond
when the sky turned
black, the air, electric.
The groundskeeper Seb
in his solo canoe,
came in the dark
and went in the dark.
A frail old man
in a green metal boat
promised to take me to shore.
But the wind
carried him away from me,
the way it seemed to carry
all the swimmers, the pond
too much mine, its old glass shattering,
my body lost, under water, under rain, lightning,
swimming, dogged in a way, but mostly choice-less,
slipping my hands over and over into the water,
noticing the absence of those close to me—
my mother, her rosary, my sister asleep,
Masami in Lima—prayers,
prayers for myself, for the woman
whose waterproof watch I'd just borrowed,
the letter I'd written earlier that day,
familial vows, random debts, ill-fated love,
these were resolved by the time
I stepped through the muck

to shore, half expecting to see
my family, Masami,
someone dear...

Instead it was New Hampshire.
I saw strangers standing there in a line,
some of them still in their bathing suits,
some waving their towels to greet me,
so many patient strangers waiting,
their anonymous arms
the most difficult kind of devotion.

LOVES MY MOTHER TAUGHT ME

The swivel stools in donut shops, buttermilk bars,
chocolate glazed, milk in cartons sipped through straws,
daffodils, geraniums, lobelia: the names of flowers.
Backyard chives, cantaloupe, yellow houses, catalogs,
paper-folding, pinafores, chocolate milkshakes, Ovaltine.
Lemon bundt cakes, rosaries, African violets, carpentry,
sharp scissors, sharper knives, genuflection, sewing machines.
Holy water, fallen leaves, petticoats, calligraphy,
scalloped brick around a tree, tissue paper, succulents.
Crescent rolls, creme rinse, almond Jello, bodices,
bus tokens, day-old bread, Christmas trees, silence.
Parmesan fans, father jokes, garden trowels, shyness.
Quiet speech, nightly prayers, leaving & amnesia,
distance, window seats, a better life, nostalgia.

PRAYER
for Maceo

Cardinal in snow, blood with wings,
fist of fire in winter sings. Sparks
from twigs of bodies touching,
heat we make for others. Elegant marks
made in secret on ether. Healing fever,
map of flaws, map of one's salvation.
Here infinity attends to measure;
the hungry find transfusion.
Birds in formation across the sky,
cave for dreaming, nest for sleep,
mist, bee's breath, tree's sigh.
Rain pouring upward, water that leaps
at the mouth of God, a drink, a scrawl,
leaf that loves the wind too much to fall.

FLAME

There was the book of poems your mother wrote,
the one I held when I was twenty, before
my house burned down (all lost), before

I knew you. Was it the mother I loved
when I read? Your body inside her
I memorized? All of the words,
sound sums in equations of fire.

Each letter a drum; I listened
and followed, listened
and followed. Sad tunes
through the trees
flaming down.

What are you?
Earth, ash, lyre,
salvage or fire?

TO BE MADE

After the day is over, we eat.
There is not much food in the cupboard.
We make noodles. We make beans.
We take all the dried things and cook them.

Crickets chirp even though it is daytime.
Not because it is rural, but because it is warm.
The air is dry. There is no rain. The earth opens up.
Crickets crawl out of the sewers and into the place.

The crickets seem to be made of twigs.
They seem to have been made by someone.
We believe they have been made by someone.

You smoke after the meal and I open the windows.
Fumes from the cars next door come in.

I want something sweet, you say
and look out at the machines.
Every day you love sugar.
Tomorrow you'll want it again.

You love oranges. Sometimes you eat
the inner skin. Pears you cut into pieces.
You make them pretty like blossoms or fans.
Our apartment is small, but I like it.

Do you want me to make the bread you like?
All three rooms will smell like cinnamon.
Maybe, you say.

There's a teaspoon of cinnamon left in the bag,
I say, *Why don't you let me.*

THE WORLD BEFORE THE WORLD

You say: *Maya...*
Sycamore Street...
painted together...

I imagine an ancient
civilization, lush trees,
an earthly renaissance.

But it's not the imaginary
I'm after. I came after
the thing called past,

that tiny globe, lit
by a pinhole you peer into.
What do you see?

Are the houses pretty?
How tall are the trees?
Is the girl's hand soft?

Let me see.

When I step close
to the hole, my eyes make it
night in the little town.

Seed-size people asleep,
no insomniacs visible.
Then you let me hold it.

I peer in, I'm so close
I worry my breath
will topple the trees,

whistle in the ears
of the sleepwalkers.
Nothing moves.

The streetlights are out,
the town has no cars.
Only sleepers in the dark

of their beds. Feverish
or resting, dreaming
or not, I can't reach them.

When I hear it
I don't know if it's
your sigh or mine...

If at last I am hearing
a breath from the town,
a sigh from a girl

with an ancient name
who dreams of a world
after this one.

ENTER THE DARK

I could not tell you
what I saw when I entered the dark,
the glittering, the carnival room.

You were there as I knew you
and as I have never known you.
Your decades of faces and hands.

Some I knew and reached out to touch.
Some were strange,
I stepped closer to them.

One hand was cold, blue as a sheep's eye.
One combed my hair
another held me.

Some of the faces knew me. Their eyes
the eyes of the neighborhood children
I chased then and shot at with shiny toy guns.

As if once long ago, I'd seen their swim suits
and bruises, slept with them soundly
on rugs of their small childhood rooms.

What was it I felt when I saw
you were so many?
Was I fooled by the carnival's tricks?

Or were your faces the guards of a hundred
more unseen worlds?
I could not tell.

But as I stood dreaming
your lifetime of faces and hands
I turned to the mirrors and saw my own.

three

RECORD PLAYER IN AN IMMIGRANT HOUSEHOLD

There is a record player, but no speakers. Father says it's no use, we can't hear the music without the proper parts. Mei and I insist, *Yes we can.* The records are 78's: children's stories, musicals, dance tunes. We love *Little Black Sambo* best.

I'm in charge of putting the record down. In imitation of him, I handle it lightly, slide its hole over the stem. The tiny tooth catches and the machine slowly lowers the record. Automatically the arm comes reaching across. We stand back and watch the needle, hear the dusty pointy crackle when it hits that is like the moment of turning on our radio. The record spins, the arm careens as the rings go around.

Someone is telling the story of *Little Black Sambo*, but the story has no place to go. Without speakers, the sound stays on the surface of the record. We put our ears as close to the spinning thing as we can without getting our hair caught. It is frustrating, not being able to hear the words without a very close, open-eared vigilance.

Then too, being the only ones to hear the sound is an awkward pleasure. It is a pleasure that makes sense to us: the forest, the tigers, the butter, all of it never existing in the room with us but somewhere else, in a country of faraway things.

A BRIEF HISTORY OF *WE* AND *US*

Whether Father was traveling, working late at the office or waiting for us in the car, we three were odd in the eyes of the world. Mother became adoptive, our nanny, our maid, a woman who happened to be standing next to us. We girls became orphans, runaways, twins. In his absence, *we* became unreadable.

It was not enough for him to sleep in the house or work in his office or wait in the car. We needed him to be in full view of the town. To mow the lawn on a sunny day, drive the car slowly with the top down, hold our hands firmly in the presence of strangers. Or else *we* disappeared.

We needed his broad face, black eyes, straight hair—on perpetual display—to explain us. Yet what did he do? He gave us food to eat and beds to sleep in; he never left us alone the way some fathers do. When he left, he wrote letters and always came back.

Made by the world, his absence would never recede. It bore the doomed sheen of the contemporary, heft of a thing that can't stop. Even today in a public place, if he leaves for a moment we feel it: the pang when *we* comes up shy of parts, when the body of *us* means nothing.

THE FATHER AND THE DAUGHTER

There once was a girl who looked so much like her father that no one in the town could tell them apart. Despite their difference in age (he was fifty-two and she was twelve) not even the artists or the architects could see that the girl's head was much lower on the horizon than her father's. The saddest part was that the girl's father was both a feared and hated man in the community. So wherever the girl went, people would either walk in the opposite direction to avoid her, or they would move aggressively toward her to throw insults.

One day, the girl went to her mother (who was white) and fell into her arms sobbing: *Mother, Mother, why are people so cruel?* At which the mother replied: *Stop crying! What is it with you men? You are like children, expecting women to see to your every need. You men are all the same!*

MUSICAL LEXICONS

If it hadn't been for our father, our mother would have loved Chinese. Despite her shyness, she pronounced the sounds with ease. To her delight, she married the languages, arranging a melodic code that my sister and I mimicked.

Wo ai ni xiao hynee, she'd say as she patted our bums. I love you little bottom. Blue*jie*. Older sister is a bird with blue wings. *Mei*flower. Younger sister is a blossom, or a ship. Her lips gave us homonym and rhyme, music and double meaning.

Our mother never spoke this way when our father was home. Perhaps with his ear there to hear her, English was the ground on which she found rest, the foreign syllables inside her mistakes waiting to happen, tests to fail. Or perhaps this was her language of love and in his presence she could not make the sounds.

Our father assumed she had forgotten her Chinese. During those rare occasions my sister and I were with him alone, he would sing in English, "You know your mother used to speak Chinese. Never practiced. Forgot everything."

NEW OLD

It is the largest sofa I have ever seen, the size of three rollercoaster seats joined together. I don't remember what it looks like underneath because soon after we move it from a stranger's house to our own, Mother sews it a cover. She takes the money Father has given her and buys the only remnant that is big enough.

The fabric is green and red polyester, its pattern has the look of capillaries or endless waves—difficult against our rust-colored carpet. The cover has one handsome feature and that is its piping, which is the color of cantaloupe and which runs the length of every edge, like a vein or a soft fence. If one could train one's eyes to look at this melon boundary without considering the sea of red and green, one could see the sofa as beautiful.

Mother sleeps on it during the day and though we are forbidden to disturb her, we always have questions. Often I sit on the carpet next to her face, waiting for her eyes to open so that I might ask her the sum of five and six or why it is some flowers have thorns and others, just smooth stems.

Her skin is the color of old sugar cubes. Her eyelashes look like the fine legs of dead insects; they respond to a breeze in the room with a twitch. I am sad for her skin. It seems as if it has never skimmed the surface of water or been touched by the sun.

She is dreaming. I think of a dream for her, a place with sea and grass and cantaloupes. I want the waves to carry her there, until I realize she will go without me. Then I want to bring her back and so I push my kneecaps into the sofa. She turns in her sleep, in the dream I have given her and as she turns I see the other side of her face, which has been pressed against the cushions.

It is a new old moment. I see the imprint of the sofa piping on her face. I see that my cantaloupe fence has made lines across her cheeks and eyelids. Sleep has left its deep signature on Mother's face without her knowing.

MOTHER'S VIOLIN

I was afraid of that violin. Mother kept it in the closet near the front door. She kept it in the darkest, furthest corner, leaned against the wall. It stood there upright, like a featureless man and I tried not to look at it whenever I opened the closet. I imagined our winter coats and rain gear, the perpetual night of the closet's interior, were merely foils for the man in the violin-shaped case. I tried to hold my eyes steady, tried to look straight ahead at the assortment of coat sleeves. But inevitably my eyes wandered down and back. The urge to see its shape, to feel a tingle of fear, overtook me. I would allow myself one glimpse: the brown and white weave of the case seemed to me the finest lattice of complications and the curve of the case a not yet formed man or worse, a woman with a little man inside.

FATHER'S VIOLIN

We have never seen it. Unlike Mother's which rests in the closet on the hardwood floor under all our coats and raingear. Its music muffled by arms of wool, collars of nylon and faux fur. Its body housed in velvet, its bow and rosin box locked in the grooves of a tailored, voluminous chamber.

Father's violin is in China. The place our classmates look for when they dig. It sleeps in a cupboard between a silver flute and a tea cup. It is buried in the yard behind the house that holds the cupboard that holds the cup. It is ash in a furrowed field—once the yard behind the house that held the cupboard that held the cup. It is somewhere in the province of Shandong, the place of "shantung" silk. We imagine its music at once spun and wild, rough and silky. Father's spinning, his roughness. His violin that makes music we have never heard.

INDECIPHERABLE GUIDE TO STRANGE BIRDS

Father keeps his calendar next to the toilet, in a wooden slot he nailed to the wall. With his pen on a string, tied to the spiral spine of the calendar, he makes notations on each of the days. A flurry of x's and o's, checks, plusses and minuses. Only the numbers are familiar. He uses the same ones we do to record his weight, once before breakfast and once before sleep. None of his bodily changes go unnoticed and all are documented. At school we learn that women may benefit from the use of calendars, but he is the only man we know to do this.

When he is gone, I go into the bathroom and look at the calendar. Its North American birds are water-stained and yet they are stranger and more vivid than the ones in our yard. The sparrows that dot our orange tree like leaves are a modest grey and the hummingbird's ruby throat is just a flash at the window. It is the red robe and black mask of the cardinal in snow that impress me. A bird so red not even the snow can freeze it. I stare at the photograph—their wedding month—and check the 26th for special markings. Nothing.

At last I turn my attention to the notations. I call Mei
to the bathroom and together we study them. We discuss
possible meanings. Food. Sleep. Exercise. Excretions.
We will never ask for a translation. We will guess
and guess and then when we are older we will forget.
Meanwhile, the calendar will be another indication of our
father's unseen clock, his well-wound mystery. We will
decipher only that every day of his life since we have
known him, his weight fluctuates from 136 to 139, resting
most days at 138, that he is a master of codes, king of all
the beautiful birds in America.

ACKNOWLEDGMENTS

Grateful acknowledgment is made to the editors of the following journals in which my poems have appeared or will soon appear, sometimes in different forms:

APA Journal: "Mother's Violin," "Musical Lexicons"
Artful Dodge: "In the Absence of Dictionaries," "Devotions"
Barrow Street: "A Picture Language"
Confrontation: "Against Einstein"
Crab Orchard Review: "Prayer"
Crazyhorse: "When the Living Say No"
Grand Street: "Dark-eyed Junco," "Possible Body"
Green Mountains Review: "The Father and the Daughter"
Hawai'i Review: "Indecipherable Guide to Strange Birds," "Another Immigrant in Love"
Indiana Review: "To the Thing Itself"
Love's Shadow: Writings by Women ed. by Amber Coverdale Sumrall (Crossing Press, 1993): "Desire"
Margie/The American Journal of Poetry: "Liars"
Massachusetts Review: "Exotic Winter," For My Father," "My Father on Poetry"
Ploughshares: "Autobiography of an Immigrant," "Trees"
Sonora Review: "To Be Made"
Spoon River Poetry Review: "Red Handkerchief," "Tender"
Sycamore Review: "The Human Part"
Texas Review: "Record Player in an Immigrant Household"
Zyzzyva: "The Vanishing"

Many thanks to the Syvenna Foundation, Cottages at Hedgebrook, the MacDowell Colony, the A Room of Her Own Foundation, UCLA's Asian American Studies Center and Institute of American Cultures, the Snazzy Writers' Workshop, the Fine Arts Work Center in Provincetown, Liberation Yoga, City Yoga, The Asian American Writers' Workshop, Blue Hen Vietnamese Kitchen in Eagle Rock, book designer Erin Shigaki and manuscript judges Eugene Gloria, Anjali Singh and Arthur Sze. Special thanks to Sue Kwock Kim and Prageeta Sharma...

To all my teachers and healers, companions in and guardians of poetry, especially Michael Burkard, Mark Doty, Mike Edwards, Kathy Garlick, David Kasdorf, Robin D.G. Kelley, Margaret Kilgallen, Paul Kolp, Robin Lewis, David Wong Louie, Valerie Matsumoto, Sarah Murphy, G.E. Patterson, Joan Stone, Adrienne Lanier Seward and Jim Trissel...

To readers Chi-Wai Au, Beth Ann Fennelly, Fanny Howe, Sharon Kraus, Suneeta Peres da Costa and Jason Zuzga for their remarkable generosity and vision...

To my friends and family...

To Mei-Mei and Maceo...

gratitude and love.

Note: The phrase "very faint, very human" *(The Human Part)* is borrowed from Michael Ondaatje.

photo: Maceo Senna

JENNIFER TSENG was born in Indiana and raised in California. She received her MA in Asian American Studies from the University of California, Los Angeles, her MFA from the University of Houston and she was twice a fellow at the Fine Arts Work Center in Provincetown. In addition to having taught Asian American Studies and Creative Writing at UCLA and Hampshire College respectively, she has taught Poetic Forms for Khmer Girls in Action in Long Beach and Poetry in Translation for the A Room of Her Own Foundation in New Mexico. Her poetry and prose have appeared in *Barrow Street, Glimmer Train Stories, Indiana Review, Ploughshares* and elsewhere. She lives in California and Massachusetts.